Sarina is a fully qualified therapist, who lives and works in the South of England. She loves travelling and exploring the world. She says that in another lifetime or if she were choosing a new career today, she would be a geologist and go digging for gems in exotic locations around the world. Although she adores the subject of recovery, the mind and the complexities of addiction, there is something to be said for losing oneself in the earth and collecting beautiful gemstones. A metaphorical idea perhaps, about the process of therapy and recovery.

I would like to dedicate the book to my mother and Alex, loved and never forgotten.

Sarina Wheatman

TWISTED WIRES

AUSTIN MACAULEY
PUBLISHERS LTD.

A CIP catalogue record for this title is available from the British Library.

ISBN 9781786937636 (Paperback)
ISBN 9781786937643 (Hardback)
ISBN 9781786937650 (E-Book)
www.austinmacauley.com

First Published (2017)
Austin Macauley Publishers Ltd.
25 Canada Square
Canary Wharf
London
E14 5LQ

Acknowledgments

I would like an acknowledgement given to Steve Stephens, "who helped me discover the truth."

Foreword

There is a song, sung by the folk singer Joan Baez in which there is a line "I have looked at life from both sides now". This is what my journey into active addiction has been about, in fact, I have looked at my life from all sides now. I have journeyed from loneliness, despair and hopelessness, to a place where I spend my time counselling and offering therapy to those who still suffer the ravages of addiction.

I knew little of alcoholism or other addictions in my youth and was certainly not taught anything about it at medical school. To me, alcohol meant fun times and a release from the pressures of a demanding and at times all-consuming job. Although I had a very adequate ability to consume alcohol, an alcoholic was someone who drank more than I did. Looking back, I can now see how I drifted later in life into being a mostly high functioning alcoholic. The fact that there was alcoholism in my family had no impact. Being a doctor, I felt absolved from such frailties in life. At the point of retirement, not only did I discover I had cancer, but my beautiful daughter was killed in a horse riding accident. I descended into active and progressive alcoholic disease, not because of these dreadful life events, but because I suffered with the genetic defect that all addicts have.

After two unsuccessful attempts at sobriety, one lasting eight months, I was coerced by my wife and family to enter into formal rehabilitation. There, I was stripped of my delusions of grandeur and nurtured into facing who and what I had become as a result of my addiction. I slowly came to realise that a life without alcohol could be full of so much genuine fun, enjoyment and fulfilment. I had taken off the imprisoning jacket of chemical addiction, and the choice of freedom came back in my life. I was at last able to see and appreciate the beauty that surrounded me.

I have made this sound easy, maybe, but it was not, and was excruciatingly painful and self-revealing. Without other people going through this with me and the remarkable skill, understanding and kindness of the staff at the clinic, this could never have happened. I am now in my seventh year of not only sobriety, but of true recovery. I have come to understand how this cunning and baffling illness works, and by retuning my thought processes and behaviour have come to live a full and rewarding life. My "Twisted Wires" have been, bit by bit, straightened out, the process is ongoing as my "isms" of behaviour still exist. It is difficult to eat just one sweet from a bag, and I still wander towards thrill seeking, but I am learning how to manage these feelings so that they do not impinge on my life or on others with whom I come into contact.

I have now retrained in counselling and addiction therapy. The poacher has now become a gamekeeper. This book has been written at a most appropriate time, when there is need for a sea change in the thinking and understanding of addictive disease and its treatment. We addicts are not hopeless people with lack of moral fibre, and this book has dispelled the myths and misconceptions surrounding addiction and its treatment. It is written by a woman of conviction, unbounded compassion and consummate skill. It is a privilege to write a forward to this book and to have been given the opportunity to add my voice to hers in the quest for better understanding of this killer disease.

Dr. Osmond Jones BACP, FDAP

Contents

Introduction

I am a recovering alcoholic/addict with over thirty years of sobriety. I have also worked in the field of addictions for over twenty-five years.

I first got sober by walking into my first Alcoholics Anonymous Meeting in 1984. I was very fortunate to walk out at the end of that first meeting never to pick up a drink or drug again. I didn't know it at the time, but walking into that first meeting was to herald the end of my using life and the beginning of a recovery. I was fairly young; I used mostly alcohol interspersed with amphetamines and occasionally when I could afford it, cocaine. I had tried cannabis and LSD, but both drugs made me feel paranoid, so didn't bother with them. I wanted to get high, I wanted to party, I wanted a social lubricant and the drugs I chose fit the bill nicely. They also helped with the crippling shyness that is the burden of many young people. What I know now, and didn't then of course, is that some drugs create different psychological states in an individual. The paranoia I felt when using cannabis had a mild effect when compared to what it is capable of doing. It can go on to trigger a complete psychological breakdown in some. There is no way of knowing who it will effect of course, so it can really be likened to playing Russian roulette. I was lucky in that my mind stayed intact, however my behaviour became increasingly erratic, dangerous and embarrassing. Like many with this addiction, as the disease progressed, I became a person I was ashamed of being. The crisis that pushed me into doing something about my using involved a relationship that was struggling to survive the behaviour that was created by addiction. The illness had not progressed to the point where seeing the "truth" about myself was impossible, so I had a motive and a reason to want to change. I had five years of clean time when I was accepted as a trainee counsellor in an in-patient facility using an abstinence-based method of treatment. I went to college, discovered I had a brain, studied, and also continued to attend AA Meetings. It was through working in rehabs and going to AA that I came to realise that I was one of the lucky ones, in as much as I had continued sobriety without any relapses. It was working in the treatment facility that I realised that relapses were a common occurrence. I am blessed, I believe, in having an enquiring mind. I wanted to know why some people relapsed and others did not. What was the secret magic ingredient?

I found there are many ingredients that make a good recovery. Whilst going to the meetings, I noticed that the people who stayed around and involved themselves in the business of recovery were the ones that remained sober. It is easy to sit in a meeting and pretend to be involved and get absolutely nothing from the experience. So I realised it is involvement that gives the staying power. This, and the job I chose, meant that I needed to understand in depth the mechanics of something called The 12 Steps that the people in the meetings spoke about, these Steps I found, are what going to meetings is really all about. Not just to stay sober myself, but to explain them to others. Simply put, they are the instructions of HOW to stay sober that were first talked about seventy years ago by the founders of Alcoholics Anonymous. To be effective in my job I needed to access the latest research; luckily, I developed a passion for this early on. Here I learnt about the mind, about neural pathways, about genetic makeup and many other interesting facts. My experience in rehab and being part of the journey of others who make it to recovery, and of those who relapse, has shown me other things that contribute to recovery and relapse. What astounds me most of all today, is how people underestimate the power of addiction. Taking risks, being blasé, cutting corners and sometimes just being plain stupid around and about substances that have the power to kill are some of the things I encounter daily. It is one thing to do these things before you educate yourself through going to meetings or getting help via a therapist. It is something else to keep doing the same things with all the knowledge you get in rehab or meetings. Jung said, when he was asked about the relapses of someone he worked with, *"that for some only a profound spiritual experience could make a difference."* This quote is found in one of the chapters of the AA Big Book. People have got tangled up with this statement and "The God Word" to such an extent that it keeps people away from the very thing that could help them. Getting a solution to addiction by attending one of the Anonymous meetings does not mean one has to get religion. Yet it is extraordinary how many people continue to believe this, and as a consequence refuse to go or stay in AA.

So I have written this book in an attempt to dispel some myths and misconceptions about the disease of addiction and the treatment that can help once diagnosed. It is written in the hope that it will reach the struggling addict out there in the world who has had enough and wants to change, or the addict who knows enough is enough and a change has to happen. It is hoped it can help direct struggling family and friends who often end up as desperate as the addicted person, not knowing where to turn to get the help they need. Perhaps it is also an attempt to look at what can be done in our society where so many people believe that the addicted person is weak willed at best and, at worst, a moral degenerate. The "twisted wires" referred to in the title describes many different aspects of the problem of addiction. It definitely refers to the thinking of an addict which is twisted in a way that makes little sense to non-addicts. But also to the logic most non-addicts have that to use or not, is a matter of choice.

My Credentials

I am a fully accredited member of The Federation of Drug and Alcohol Professionals (FDAP). I have worked in various treatment centres both in England and Europe, always using what is known as the "abstinence method" with my patients. This method is also known as The 12 Steps and ascribes to the philosophy of Alcoholics Anonymous and other 12 Step fellowships. I have been privileged to work with many fine therapists over the years to whom I owe a huge debt of gratitude. I also have worked with and been part of many amazing recoveries over the years. There have also been people along the way who have not got well, who have rejected this type of therapy, but the vast majority of people I have been involved with over a span of twenty-five years have recovered from this most debilitating of afflictions. Is it a disease, an illness? This question has been at the forefront of every argument from every detractor of the 12 Steps for eons, or at least ever since I started to take notice of the question. I hope my book goes some way in clearing up some of the doubt. If this occurs, then perhaps we can then get on and spend more time on the business of recovery. Of course I not only use the 12 Steps in my work, but use them personally in my own life. They have saved my life, and go on giving me a quality of life I could never have dreamt about in throes of my addiction. Death is the end result of untreated addiction and the numbers of deaths are way beyond the reported statistics. This war on addiction, this persecution of addicts and alcoholics, does not have any victors. The addicts behave intolerably, lives and families are destroyed, the hospitals cannot cope, the police are not making inroads. Surely it is time to take stock and try to find another way. I believe a shift in perception about what we are dealing with may open up avenues for better education, better treatment, better outcomes.

There is a sea change in the wind. People, countries and law makers are more inclined to want to discover other methods than the ones they already have to try to combat this "war on addiction". Incarceration, stiffer penalties and in some countries even the death penalty have not curbed the explosion of addicts in our world. My argument is that if it is an illness, a disease, how is it that we punish the people who have it? In some forward-thinking countries there already exist modalities where the legalisation is changing. Decriminalisation doesn't mean carte blanche, but it does mean a change needs to take place. Change and reform for systems that obviously do not work. Once upon a time, alcohol was prohibited in America. The illegal industry that sprang up around it all shows that there was a need, and there will always be an industry to provide for the need. My hope is that we would all rather be part of a solution than to continue to living with the problem.

Chapter 1
There is a Way

Addictions are on the rise, science and psychology have advanced, and there are so many smart intelligent people, but solutions seem to elude us. Why?

Displaced people, poverty, parents with little time. We all know those awful stories of unwanted kids, or of families that have no time. Yet some addicts, have fabulous everythings; so the answer is not in our history, although it certainly plays a part in who we become. The answer? Maybe a vague sense of discontent, a feeling, an alienation. In some it manifests as phobia and they retreat into self-made prisons; in some it develops into mania, making them louder more insistent on being heard. Introverts, extroverts, male, female, rich or poor, of course there is no pattern to inform or warn. Whatever it is, addicts all begin with the genetic makeup that makes them different to others in the world. Statistics tell us one in ten of the population have an addiction. (This is most assuredly a conservative estimate.) Addicts, moral degenerates, stubborn selfish people. Or unwell individuals with a disease?

We have to choose which camp to believe, some say to choose to believe addiction is an illness is a cop out.

"Surely, it's you who does it, takes the stuff, lies, steals and acts like a maniac?" There's no doubt, the addicted person in action is revolting, becoming a monster as the disease progresses. Hurting self and anyone else brave enough to stay close. Yet the strange thing is that if we can believe in the disease concept, there is a possibility that individuals can stop, can get better and can recover.

Addiction was described as a disease over seventy years ago by the men who started Alcoholics Anonymous, but today there are more institutions who have publicly announced it as so, The World Health Organisation and The Medical Association being two bodies that have documented this idea. Confusion reigns however, as detractors cannot get past the idea that this is a cop out. But why is the thinking like this? Even addicts themselves sometimes believe this. Insanity is a word often used to describe the actions of the addicted person and certainly some behaviours can only be described as such.

The person who leaves their kid alone at home to go and score, the driver who drinks and drives whilst knowing it is wrong, the pupil who misses school because getting high is more appealing than exams, the person who gambles the mortgage payment away. The violence and mayhem on a Saturday nights High Street and the overstretched ER in hospitals around the globe. All compelling reasons to use the word insanity, but it is not *the actions* of the addict that should be concentrated on, but *the thinking.* The thinking behind the actions, the doing over and over again, not expecting the same results. It is this thinking that can be described as insane. There is compelling evidence today that shows that the neural pathways in an addict's brains are different. The research shows that what appears to some as "choice" becomes "need or instinct" to the addict. Addicts have flawed thinking, and it is this that causes so many problems. No-one likes to believe they are different, and it is this that is seen as the cop out. Yet as the incidences of addiction grow in our world, maybe just maybe, if the arguments stopped, we could find the solution. There is no doubt that human beings can learn, and relearn, can make changes, break habits, recover from addictions. This is proved over and over again in recovering addict's lives; yet because relapse is so common, and relapse is often done with a bang and not a whimper, it is the *behaviour* and not the *thinking* that is examined.

We have all seen the media stories of gifted people getting into trouble with alcohol or drugs or some other addiction and we have gone on the rehab trail with some of them. We have wondered why, when this or that person seems to have it all they choose to behave in the way they do. We can feel empathy, sadness or pity when someone has their life cut short because of untreated addiction. The stories, unfortunately, are endless and the behaviour of those caught in the grip of addiction become increasingly bizarre. Sympathy eventually can turn to impatience or contempt. What is perhaps not known, are the endless repeats of these media stories that happen in the lives and families of the public at large. The impatience is the same however, *"For goodness sake, why don't they just stop doing this to their lives?"* The truth is that to recover from an addiction is enormously difficult. It means lifestyles have to change, friends and loved ones have to come aboard or be left behind if they can't. The individual has to embark on a journey that will transform their thinking. This, of course, is not easy. Some are not prepared to make the changes, and some underestimate what has to be done. The twisted thinking that accompanies addiction is complex, heart-breaking, infuriating and very difficult to change.

Twisted Wires?

Spend any time at all in the company or world of the addict, and the term twisted wires can be easily understood when describing what happens in their lives and the lives of family or anyone who gets close. Twisted wires refer to many aspects of this complicated disease. To watch or witness the self-destruction that is present in many addicts' lives appears to on-lookers as incomprehensible. It is described as madness certainly, and the 12 Step Anonymous movement talks about a return to sanity. But it is not the *behaviour* of the addict that should be focused on, although it seems pretty insane a lot of the time, but it is the *thinking* behind the behaviour that causes most of the problem. This is more easily seen and understood when looking at the many relapses that occur in this illness. The fact that someone can be sober or clean for long lengths of time and then "suddenly" relapse has baffled many, including addicts themselves. Why would someone who to all intents and purposes has got their life back on track suddenly decide it is okay to use again? There are many reasons why relapses occur, but the most compelling and easy to comprehend is that the fact that "addiction as an incurable illness" was never fully understood. As with some other illnesses the person who has it needs to manage it, and so it is with addiction. To gain any length of clean time or sobriety takes a fundamental change in the way someone leads their life. The people mixed with, the places frequented, things done. What is sometimes missed or not understood, is that this change in lifestyle needs to continue indefinitely. Some addicts get blasé after some clean time is achieved, and some get careless. Some go as far as to believe that because some clean time or sobriety has now been achieved, they will be able to control their use again. They are back in charge, they think, but they never are.

Euphoric recall is also a persuasive and powerful reason many do not succeed in achieving lasting sobriety. This euphoric aspect to addiction is what makes it so compelling to addicts; it makes a dull day bright, emotional pain forgotten, boredom flies away, life is exciting and the world is there for the taking. The fact that the brightness fades, the pain comes back and boredom returns does not dispel the desire for instant solutions. Take something, and all is well with the world. The addict learnt that the first time they used and is the thing that endures despite overwhelming evidence that the world is crashing around their feet.

It is hard to change; harder still when everyone we mix with has to be part of the change. Until the disease concept is understood, non addicts who have been around and witnessed the destructive way of the addict can quite conceivably be too hurt or too angry to want to be part of the change. Many relationships do not survive, of course, because the damage has been so profound. Because of the misinformation about addictive disease, what should be common knowledge is not, and so society on the whole does not want to be part of the change. When the belief in society is that it is self-inflicted illness and that choice is the operative word then, of course, no-one wants to be part of the change; the addict is to blame, the addict needs to sort it all out. If only they would stop and stay clean all would be well. Of course they need to stop, but it cannot be achieved alone.

Twisted wires can be seen in all aspects of this disease, the way the addict thinks, the way they behave, the way they relapse. It refers to society's views on the subject; the rage it inspires in so many. It refers to the confusion that exists in treating the illness. In the way that drugs and alcohol are viewed. How it is criminalised, how much money is involved in the illegal trade, how there seems to be no solutions. Yet millions have found recovery. There is a solution; but first perhaps, the whole business of twisted thinking needs to be aired. What is it about this disease that inspires so much venom? The arguments about it are endless. Because the non-addicted person drinks "normally" and this type of drinking is not out of control, perhaps the view is, "well, I can control myself, why can't they", which of course shows no comprehension about addiction. Everyone says they understand it, however the attitudes in society about addiction would suggest otherwise. Addiction only affects a percentage of the population. It skips generations, exists for instance in one twin and not the other, in one sibling in a family of six, etc. etc. There seems to be no rhyme or reason when the addictive gene is doled out. The disease is only noticed when the behaviour, usually destructive has commenced. By the time it is noticed, it will have been developing for some time. By the time it is noticed, denial will have set in, and the whole sad game commences. The compulsion to use grows ever stronger, the obsession takes over, and lies, secrecy and destruction are the name of the game.

Chapter 2
Somewhere Else

For as long as memory serves, we yearn to be somewhere,
Anywhere else,
Here, the present, is never able to match that other place,
That somewhere, that anywhere else.
The now, in its compartmentalised zones,
Is dull, is wrong, is no-where
We want to be.
For as long as memory serves, somewhere
Has been anywhere else.

So, it could be said, "Somewhere else" is what addicts seek. In some, the substance or addictive behaviour that is chosen seems to offer a shortcut to feeling fulfilled, at peace, or satisfied. It works initially in the euphoric highs that some addictions give, but eventually the high cannot be sustained without more, and the more is never enough. People with advanced addictions are the modern-day lepers, shunned, despised, and very much misunderstood.

But we shouldn't misunderstand. This isn't about letting the addict off the hook, or about a soft approach.

There is no place for this type of attitude where addiction is concerned. Addicts themselves don't really want to stop unless there is no more choice. Denial is a word often used in relation to addiction. Denial serves the addicted mind so well. It makes the negative consequences of drugged behaviour, someone, and something else's fault. Or it convinces that this time it will be different, control is possible. The unpredictability of it all makes it so hard to understand. Sometimes it is possible to have just one, sometimes it is possible not to take it too far; but inevitably, if addiction is present, loss of control will occur. It is in these times that the rest of the world looks on in disbelief. It is after these times the addict mostly feels shame, guilt and remorse, and will desperately attempt to find the solution. But as the solution for the addicted person is to use, life will take on a "groundhog day" quality, with ever increasing problems.

Somewhere else – please!

In my own life, I was a very shy, introverted child and teenager, the type of person that would blush if anyone looked at her; it was painful and I hated feeling this way. When I discovered alcohol and later amphetamines, I loved the effect they gave me. I went from this shy, introverted girl, to the life and soul of the party; the fact that I very often blacked out and couldn't remember what I did seemed a price I was willing to pay. I was fortunate that for most of this destructive using I was protected by family, friends or boyfriends, so nothing too terrible happened. I realise today, especially because of the work I do, that others are not so lucky. These blackouts which I casually accepted as part of my using life, are in fact dangerous in many ways, and one of the first visible signs of addiction. Accident and Emergency rooms are littered with people after a night out, others are prey to all sorts of "nasties" that inhabit our world. There are lots of young people who feel socially inadequate who don't use substances, and for others who do, some will grow out of it, as of course it is a part of growing up. Addicts, though, who discover this solution to fix the way they feel cannot "grow out of it". For me, the effects were profound and powerful. I courted this "somewhere else, someone else" feeling. As the disease progressed and my behaviour became more problematic, there seemed no way out, I had never learned how to negotiate life without substances, and life without substances was intolerable. I was on the merry-go-round and did not know how to get off. In the early years of my addiction, I didn't even want to get off, I liked the high, the buzz, the living on the edge. Or at least I thought I liked it. The "day of reckoning" came however, and when it did I despised myself, but getting off seemed impossible.

If the addiction is not too far advanced there may be moments of clarity, a little moment of truth where addicts can see themselves as they truly are. If this occurs, then this is the moment that recovery could begin. The addict with the malfunctioning brain, of course, needs the right type of help. Alcoholics Anonymous got it right all those years ago. Even today, despite much misunderstanding through the years, and many detractors, it is the single most successful approach for addictions. But because of the misunderstandings (it's a cult, don'tcha know?), myths and other absurdities, it is often discounted. More of those twisted wires? Everything about this subject seems to be twisted. The legendary hard drinkers are courted until the problems start. Most social situations involve alcohol and or drugs of some sort or another.

Nobody bats an eye until the problems start. Shame about the situation only appears when someone wants to go for help, then The Anonymous part of the AA movement really comes into its own. We are stealthy about going into rehab, we keep this quiet or are ashamed to tell. The shame about being seen going into an AA meeting far outweighs the shame of stumbling around drunk in the street, or waking up beside someone whose name you don't know, getting into a car and driving whilst drunk, or fighting the ones you love in a drunken blackout. Crazy scenarios with no answers. Of course addicts hate themselves when reality arrives. Of course the onlooker is appalled. Shame is a correct feeling at this point, but how sad that shame usually intensifies when the moment to ask for help has arrived. Another example, perhaps, of Twisted Wires?

Chapter 3
Moments of Truth

The fact that addictions exist and have a genetic component should be taught in schools, but sadly it is not. "Choice" and "just say no", are the usual advice. So is it any wonder we are losing this particular battle and addictions are on the rise? How can we just say no with a brain that is wired differently? This fact should be something taught in schools, this is the truth about addiction. Truth, they say, sets us free, and certainly if the truth about addiction were more widely known, perhaps many would not fall into its trap or if already in it, find the way out more easily. But there are other things about truth that can give us answers.

There are snapshots of time in people's lives, moments where the truth is unavoidable. Addicts do have them, they wish to avoid them, but they do exist. A view of self that is without deception, of behaviour that can no longer be denied. It is in these moments when, if the right kind of intervention takes place, a recovery could happen. These moments are fleeting; however, this is where the choice is, to really see, understand and act, or to deny, excuse and do nothing. So several things need to happen at once for a change to happen. The individual needs to see the truth, to want things to change and then have the opportunity to illicit a change. It is this moment, fleeting and unclear, that can be described as "a rock-bottom". It used to be that the gutter was thought of as an alcoholic's rock bottom, but any time they say "enough is enough" can be that time.

As an example, *I had known something was wrong with my using and behaviour for quite some time. I had run away to Australia to escape my mother's disapproval and despair. Things of course were no better 12,000 miles away, and the freedom my new life gave me, in fact speeded up the progression of the disease. I began to notice the street people of Sydney, bag ladies they were called, who wheeled their possessions around in shopping trollies, and seemed old beyond years. I remember thinking "there but for the grace of something go I." An odd thought for a young person to have, with friends, a job and place to live. Yet I also had visions of myself as that blousy bleached blonde propped up on a bar stool, smoking and hoping the stranger next to her would buy her the next drink. Premonition, fear, warning? Who knows, but I saw myself in these roles, and knew I did not wish for them to become reality.*

Addicts end up in rehab or one of the Anonymous meetings, always because of some sort of crisis. Few go easily and risk the wrath and scorn of the world, and that's how twisted this all is. The shame about addiction comes when seeking help rather than the act itself. Using is seen as cool or fun; it is used as a social lubricant, and almost seen as a rite of passage in some young people. Addicts often feel a deep sense of shame and self-loathing if seen to be going to meetings or treatment. The behaviours may have hit new lows, of course, and the loved ones, who have put up with all sorts of craziness long after they should, have lost patience or belief that change can happen. So it is more twisted thinking at work here, that the shame accompanies walking into a meeting! But, however it comes, recognition that there is a problem and that denial won't cut it anymore, followed by an acceptance, no matter how begrudging, is how recovery starts. The crisis that enables *this moment of truth* could be anything, from being arrested for drunk driving and ending up in a cell overnight, some kind of health crisis, losing a job or a relationship or a hundred thousand other ways where a loss of dignity occurs. What has to be remembered by everyone is that no matter the indignities of this particular moment, there is always a worse place to get to. The progression of the disease assures us of this fact.

In Meetings or in Treatment, addicts are informed that they need abstinence in order to succeed. Abstinence is sometimes impossible without medical help, not only impossible, but in fact very dangerous. Devastation can occur when the body and mind are suddenly deprived of the thing that until now has been the solution, friend, comforter and answer to all life's discomfort and problems. To stop doing something suddenly which has become habitual is difficult, and in the case of substances and addictions, it can be lethal. As someone with an addiction to alcohol, for instance, progresses in their illness, the effects on the body are easy to notice. Advanced alcoholism and drug addictions sees all kinds of problems, such as compromised physical health, everything from raised liver counts to complete system breakdown. What is not always visible is the psychological devastation. In someone with a gambling addiction, losses, sometimes huge, are seen as the problem, but the real problem is the repeating over and over again of the same action to make things better. "*This time it will be different. I will win and all my troubles will be over.*" There are many types of addictions, from the well-documented alcohol and illegal drug problems, as well as addiction to prescription medications, gambling, sexual compulsions, legal highs, and over the counter medications, relationships, workaholism, exercise addiction, a myriad of eating disorders, gaming on the Internet, spending, nicotine addiction, and the list goes on. The progression of the addiction is what makes them visible, noticeable and sometimes deadly. Addicts fear stopping, detox and abstinence. The inability to cope physically, mentally and emotionally is a strong deterrent to stopping. The addiction is a powerful aid to life, for some, it is the solution to life's ills; without it, the addict does not know how to cope. The addiction is also a powerful destroyer of life, but finding ways to cope without it seem impossible. The addict does not understand this, family members do not understand this, and the world will not tolerate it. With all this in the mix, is it any wonder that relapse is so dominant? Underestimating the illness is common from beginning to end. If addiction could be viewed universally as an illness that was primary, chronic, progressive and fatal, an illness that had no cure but could be managed much like diabetes, perhaps we could look at addiction in a new and workable way. Perhaps prevention and/or solutions to addiction would not seem so impossible. Alcoholics Anonymous was one of the first to use the term illness and disease when describing Alcoholism. This was in the thirties, and it wasn't just lay people who made these pronouncements, but a well-known doctor of his time. A letter he wrote is printed in the Alcoholics Anonymous Book (also known as The Big Book). The American Medical Association also published statements relating to addiction to alcohol and drugs as a disease. Since then, people the world over have either agreed or disagreed. This remains a contentious subject. Addicts are often viewed as criminals rather than sick people, with many repeat offenders incarcerated. This is another area where the term twisted wires could fit. Many people have opinions on this subject, people argue incessantly. Drug addiction is seen as different to Alcoholism. Why should this be so? Narcotics Anonymous in their meetings describe alcohol as just another drug. The World Health Organisation has stated that if Alcohol were discovered today, it would be a class A Drug. Alcohol, of course, is legal which perhaps explains why it is viewed as different, yet more people die because of this drug than any other. It is indeed a political hot potato. It is interesting to research the origins of why drugs and addicts are seen as criminal. How this came about could be the subject of another book. However, when I advocate treating addicts rather than imprisoning them, I do not intend to imply we should "molly coddle" people. Untreated addiction of any kind is dangerous and the effects of this in our society could be viewed as catastrophic. "The war on drugs" with its ever increasing consequences is not working. The prisons are full, the laws are strict, yet this appears to be making little difference. People still experiment, get hooked and the cycle goes on. **IF** we had a society where addiction was understood, **IF** people stopped thinking addiction was just a matter of banning/eradicating the substance or behaviour, maybe, just maybe we could reduce the lives

37

ruined or lost. We could concentrate on educating the youth of today, our next generation, or providing more treatment to help those already in trouble. The criminal aspect that surrounds our drug culture, of course, is a huge problem, but just as in the days of prohibition in America when Alcohol was that banned substance, what grew around those attitudes were the mobsters, the black markets, etc. I am not naïve enough to think there is a quick solution, but something needs to change, and maybe the change that is needed is in societies' attitudes and the way **WE THINK** about addicts and addictions, and definitely what treatments work and what more can be made available to those that look for help or for their loved ones. There are many amazing books and films that have been written about how the current thinking about drugs and alcohol have come about. They are easily available to anyone with an interest in the subject. I have listed some of the titles in the reference section of this book and would urge anyone with an interest in this subject to read and enlighten themselves as to why the status quo is as it is. There are all sorts of reasons why this war on addiction is not being won. But this is another subject, for another book, another time. My focus remains on how to detangle some of the twisted wires in individuals who want to get clean and/or sober.

Chapter 4
Beginnings and Endings

To begin a recovery there must be an end to using. Of course, simple. So simple it is often missed. The using has become such an integral part of the individual's life that until the idea of stopping can be contemplated, recovery will not occur. In Recovery, the concept of stopping the use is introduced as stopping the fight. The moments of truth, of course, are needed here as reasons to persuade the addict this is a good idea. Medically assisted detoxes are introduced when other solutions have failed. These are essential for some, as detox is the most dangerous time for a compromised physical state. But simply removing the substance or stopping the using behaviour alone should not be viewed as recovery. This is **THE** huge underestimation that sabotages more addicts than anything else. Just stopping will not do anything except stop the deterioration in mind and body or bank balance temporarily. Medically assisted detoxes are great but only if accompanied by the psychological assistance and education about the disease that addicts need. Abstinence, of course, will only be tolerated as a solution if the disease concept is accepted; without this acceptance, then total abstinence will appear to be unnecessary or too hard core.

The idea that it will be possible to use again is, of course, the obsession of most addicts. Many relapses happen for just this reason. Either the disease concept was never really understood, or the passage of time has served to "prove" to the addict that they are really okay now. When someone stops the destructive using behaviour, then it is the beginning of recovery. It is not all that needs to happen because this illness is more complex than that. The illness affects mind, body and soul. It is fairly easy to comprehend the physical deterioration that occurs with people with advanced addiction, harder to understand that it is progressive. So someone, right at the start of this downward spiral, will be having physical symptoms which should be acknowledged. The mind and actions of a drunk or drugged individual is easy to comprehend as being problematic, but the illness is present when the individual is not drunk or drugged, and it is this that makes it difficult to understand. The illness can be seen in the actions and choices a person makes about the addiction, when to all intents and purposes they are clean and sober. It is the decisions that the individual makes despite having countless examples of the destructive things that happen when using. To the non-addict, it is a choice, to the addict, it is not that simple. The peculiar blindness that addicts have is called denial. A good definition of this odd phenomenon is "sincerely believing our own lies". The lie of addiction is that "this time it will be under control," or "one won't hurt," or "I'm better now." The lie continues, of course, getting progressively more dangerous as the disease also progresses.

Chapter 5
Stopping the Fight

Once addicts see the truth and decide that the destruction of their lives cannot go on, then what to do about it is the next thing that must be considered. Detox certainly, but also education is needed about the many layers of this illness. The best place to learn is in one of the Anonymous meetings or Rehab. This is where most addicts go for help and where the concept of addiction as an illness and how to manage it is introduced. Managed in the same way diabetes needs to be managed. There are many illnesses that cannot be halted, stopped or cured by choice, or will-power, but this is always used as an example of why addiction is not really a disease. What has to be understood is that addiction NEVER goes away, there is no cure for it, yet addicts, once they understand some of their limitations, can live healthy productive lives. Not fair, say some, still thinking that addiction is a choice. It is no more a choice than any other illness. There is a genetic precursor to the condition which needs certain things for it to develop. Much like many other illnesses really! Perhaps the rage of those who do not have it is because it looks so self-indulgent, so much *fun,* and is triggered by the taking of a substance that not everyone takes, or of a behaviour that not everyone does. Yet the taking of substances or acting in a way that provides pleasure or gratification is as old as mankind. The problems only arise when an individual cannot control the using. At the start of anyone's using, do they know this? Of course not. Because the using at the start, although initially not destructive or heavy is what triggers it all in some individuals. The progression of the disease is what **shows** the problems. The fun stuff? Well, that is usually fleeting, trouble almost always accompanies long-term addiction.

Stopping the fight means admitting, accepting and acknowledging that something is wrong with **SELF.** That what is wrong is nobody else's fault. That what is wrong is not caused by anything else. Addicts may be using because they feel depressed, or partners have left, or money is tight. Using makes these things easier to bear, offers a temporary solution, but in recovery, addicts learn that these other things need attention of a different kind. Depression needs to be medically treated and the reasons for the things that go wrong in life need to be dealt with. Addicts have to learn that using will never sort them out. As to the fun stuff, when reality is examined, few continue to believe that anyone is having fun. The euphoric highs experienced when the substances are first taken do not stay the same. More and more of the substance needs to be taken for it to continue to give the feeling desired until in the end, the using is often just to feel normal, or to get the day started, or to stop the shakes. That old drunk on a park bench, drinking from a bottle hidden in a brown paper bag, is everyone's idea of what an alcoholic is. What has to be learned, understood and remembered, is that person did not start out that way. They ended up that way and what we are witnessing is the physical manifestation of a progressive illness.

Accepting Help

Stopping the fight means accepting that the solutions to this problem cannot be achieved alone. If it were possible, it would already have happened. In the Anonymous meetings it is known as the First Step. Acknowledgment of the true problem. Many addicts believe that they use because... The reason can be anything, of course, but the truth is much more complex and the addict has to stop using in order to find out what is really wrong. The drinking, the drugging, the gambling or overeating etc. are all ways in which the addict copes with the way they feel. At first the addiction gave a sense of well-being or euphoria which is powerful and compelling. It is the progression of the disease which causes and shows the problems. Addicts need to use more and more to gain the effect they crave; it is never enough, and the mind, body and soul of the addicted person begin to deteriorate. Acceptance of help from others is crucial. Addicts can never really accept the help on offer until they accept the problem. The addicted individual tries all sorts of things to use and not have the "bad" things happen. They start every time believing that this time they will have it under control, and it won't get out of hand. Over and over again this illusion is shattered, but the insanity of this disease shows in the belief that endures, this time it will be different. The word surrender is used often when talking about recovery from addiction. There is no possibility of accepting help if surrender does not happen. There is no possibility of being helped if the problem remains one of depression, or any of the other serious mental health issues, that addicts can also have. The addict has to surrender to the fact that the using is the problem and no amount of manipulation will enable control to return. Surrendering and accepting help is demoralising, and it doesn't feel good; this moment in time happens usually because of some sort of crisis. The moment goes again so the help that is required can only happen in a brief window of time. If they go to AA or to a therapist, or to a doctor, they may learn some truths about what has been going on; they stand a chance of getting well. If addiction as a disease was more widely accepted and the true nature of this devastating illness was discussed more openly, perhaps the recovery rates would be higher, more people would seek help and not be so fearful of the stigma attached to addictions. Addicts are often described as being weak willed, however, the opposite is actually the truth. Therapists all know in rehab that unless surrender happens, a patient/client cannot be "forced" to change in the way that is needed for a recovery to occur. There is a saying associated with alcoholics and addicts which is that they are "self-will run riot". These three little words describes the early recovery process very well. It also explains why it is so hard to break through denial and stop doing the things that will ultimately lead to some sort of destruction or trouble.

Chapter 6
Surrender

Addicts are often accused of being weak-willed, but the reverse is actually true. Without surrender, there is no way an addict will let anyone help. Or have the humility to do the things that will be suggested. Surrender – Wave the white flag! Stop getting into the boxing ring! Give in! Let go! **So easy to say, so hard to do.** So how is it done?

Surrender is not just something you do with the mind, but something done with your heart and your mind. It is felt at the core of your being, where shame, remorse and sorrow reside. When one truly surrenders, you have access to these feeling memories. It is this that serves as one of the defences against using again. Although shame and remorse are hard feelings to bear, they are absolutely needed when starting this recovery process. They cannot remain in the forefront of consciousness for too long, otherwise people would go crazy, but, the ability to remember the last drunk and the mayhem that accompanied it is an important beginning in this journey back to sanity. Here is another clue as to what needs to occur in the addict's thinking; remembering the last *drunk* as opposed to the last *drink* in the case of alcoholism enables the individual to acknowledge the mayhem that ensued in the last binge, and not just the good feelings that the first few drinks created.

In some ways the process of surrender is already occurring if the addict is in a meeting or Rehab. But the problem is that recovery doesn't continue unless some stringent changes are made. It has been said that humility is needed to give in and accept help. Why is it presumed that just because the using has stopped, that is the answer? It is just the beginning. What has to happen next is a series of big and small changes to the way life has been lived. The addict doesn't know what needs to change, otherwise they would have already done it. Several things need to occur to start this process.

Ask for help… A professional, or sober individuals in the meetings.

Listen to the experts… People who know what needs to be changed.

Do what is suggested… **Now.**

Right here, right now, the decision about what is believed has to be sorted. This can only occur if acceptance about the disease concept can be made. Without this, the need for abstinence will not be believed. The need for continued abstinence will not be accepted. Recovery will only occur/start if the addict stops using. The destructive part will reappear as soon as the addict uses again. The illness **CANNOT** be cured. As soon as the addict starts using again, the illness re-activates into its destructive mode. This will occur no matter the length of abstinence, be it seven days, seven weeks, seven years or more. It is this one small but deadly fact about addiction that derails many. Remember the brain that is wired differently? Addiction is all about the brain. It is made up of several different regions that control different areas of functioning. The brain stem keeps critical symptoms like breathing going, and the cerebral cortex processes sensory information and controls thinking and decisions. We have a built-in reward system called the limbic system, and this encourages us to do things we must do for survival such as eat or procreate, by making it pleasurable, which in turn encourages us to do it again. To create this pleasure feeling, the brain releases neurotransmitters which are chemical messengers. Drugs and addictive behaviour cause effects, either by masquerading as a natural transmitter or they trigger the excessive release of the neurotransmitters, the most common being Dopamine. It is released in intense quantities, more than in natural activities, so that when the brain realizes how much it is rewarded for indulging in the addiction, the motivation to use becomes greater. With time, the motivation to enhance this process is all encompassing. The brain knows it doesn't have to activate the pleasure centres with its own Dopamine but relies on the drug or behaviour to activate the feeling of normality or happiness. The brain pushes for more and more so that the individual starts to feel bad if they don't indulge the addiction; craving occurs as the brain waits for the feeling it wants; withdrawal is a symptom of addiction that occurs as the brain waits for things to go back to normal. The brain tries to cope with the abnormal situation, which means the brain has to adapt and continue to adapt as long as the drugs are taken. The more changes made, the less it wants to change back. Hence the difficulty in getting clean. However, the brain can relearn how to navigate life differently if the addict continues to abstain it gets easier and easier to stay clean. This process must be remembered and steps must be taken to keep the addiction in its dormant stage or the addict's brain will once again focus on the need and pleasure and forget about consequences. Cravings are almost always present at the start of a recovery; they must be *managed* with medication in some cases, as well as with psychological help. The intensity will decrease. They may come and go, and the addict needs help to manage them. This is as true after seven years as it is after seven days. The desire to use can return at any time, but especially in times of high emotional stress. It is this that needs to be understood and managed, and why the addict has to stay focused on recovery. It is why addicts are told over and over not to go it alone. Left to their own devices, the addict loses focus very quickly. Once focus is lost or waning, then risky behaviour is enacted, and before you know it, the cravings return. Triggers can be anywhere in anything. Alone, it seems, the addict has no defences adequate enough against the next using spell. It is this behaviour that is so confusing to onlookers, from stone-cold sober the using behaviour is re-enacted and the trouble begins again. The behaviour doesn't make sense to anyone. However, it is the thinking that is at fault, and of course how can anyone examine the thoughts of an individual, especially of someone who wants to hide and be secretive about behaviour that everyone around him wants him to cease?

Chapter 7
How to Stay Focused

Staying focused, as already described, is the hard part. Initially the crisis that has propelled the addict into seeking help is sufficient to motivate them to go to an AA meeting or seek out a professional. Any assessment of an addiction should include the basic introduction to addiction as a disease. Anonymous meetings do this in an indirect way which makes the impatient addict miss it so often. Some addicts go to rehab having tried a meeting and not found it to be helpful; good rehabs will show how invaluable the meetings can be once they learn how to navigate them. Staying focused is one of the reasons for getting help and continuing to go to meetings. Let's assume that the addict is now dry or has stopped the addictive using behaviour. Many, including the addicts themselves, are convinced that this is all that needs to happen. Yet as the many relapses show, that is not true. The disease never goes away, and it can lie dormant, sometimes for years. It can re-activate particularly in times of high emotional stress. What the addict needs to learn very early on is that they are not at fault for having the illness, they are, however, responsible for maintaining recovery and that means taking care of self. Staying focused is part of this maintenance. Early on, it is easy to understand the need for help, but months or years down the line people become blasé about the power of addiction and the need for help. Humility needs to remain for the recovering person who is ten months or ten years in recovery to understand and accept that they continue to need help to process thoughts and feelings.

Addicts have flawed thinking. The disease never goes away. If this can be understood, then to believe an addict will be okay after stopping the using for a period of time can be seen for what it is. Just another way that twisted logic gives power to this disease.

Taking care of self means addicts need to learn about the disease first and foremost. They need to accept help. They need to stay focused. The Anonymous groups are successful in introducing like-minded people to each other. A fellow addict will understand the flawed thinking in another, the bizarre behaviour and the dangers of triggers. If an addict has found their way out of their own private hell, then helping someone else stay out of hell, often seen as an act of generosity, is actually one way individuals have found to stay clean and sober. It is the give and take nature of recovery that makes AA successful. When someone ten years in recovery aids someone who is new, they are reminded of how it was and perhaps could be again. So they are reminded to keep life simple and uncomplicated, to stay honest, and that the most important element of their life is to stay clean and sober.

Chapter 8
Anonymous Meetings versus Rehab

The way to learn about the disease is from others who have the disease, which is why the Anonymous meetings are such a good resource. Being able to get to a meeting, to understand how they work and then apply them to self is crucial, and it is the hard part. Many people try them in desperation and for many reasons do not "get it". The "old fashioned" feel of the meetings or the "cult-like" language are often cited as the reasons for the disconnect. However, anyone who has been able to stay sober/well using the meetings will tell a different story.

Alcoholics Anonymous was the first type of meeting started in 1935, but since then many other addictions have been treated in the same way, all with their own meetings. Although they are all similar in the way the treatment works, there are subtle differences in some types of addiction. Today, as well as Alcoholics Anonymous, there exists Cocaine Anonymous, Marijuana Anonymous, Narcotics Anonymous, Nicotine Anonymous, Debtors Anonymous, Gambling Anonymous, Overeaters Anonymous, Co-dependants Anonymous, Al-Anon, Sex and Love Addicts Anonymous and more. Old Fashioned?

AA meetings were started as an attempt by those early pioneers of this recovery method to reach more people who were suffering with alcoholism. Up until this time, over seventy years ago, there was little for the addict except institutions, jail, and the locked wards of hospitals. It was discovered that like-minded people who got together to talk about how they were managing to stay sober actually served to help. The language in some of the literature reflects the times. Translating and understanding it is crucial. Cringe-making, say some, psychobabble, say others. Perhaps the misinformed should talk to the alcoholic who has remained sober, rather than the people who have been unable to. The easy availability of drugs and alcohol, more money and with younger and younger individuals and their increasing "freedoms", have all made the rise in addictions explode. The type of drug and quantities used fast track the progression of the illness; perhaps this is the reason that some who seek out the Anonymous meetings for help cannot understand it. The brain and thinking of an addict, already wired differently to begin with, becomes more and more compromised as the disease progresses. Yet the addict does not believe this. So if the addict does not believe it, how or why should anyone else? Twisted wires indeed.

Rehab

Professional help is often the only way to proceed if meetings have not worked. It is said that Rehab and/or therapy can give the addict a fast track into the knowledge needed to get and stay well. Knowledge that takes months to acquire in meetings can be gained in weeks in rehab where the sole focus will be on the individual, their particular need, and where specific education about the disease and recovery will be taught.

Therapeutic work will begin the job of enabling the addict to take a close look at self. The denial that up to now has stopped the addict from seeing the true extent of the problem is stripped back and the addict will be encouraged to examine the way they have thought, felt and behaved.

Self-indulgent, some say. *All that time spent on you. The selfish monster that has done and said all those horrible things. Why should you get all the attention, what about us?*

They say an addict will adversely affect at least six other people as the disease progresses. So the damage is sometimes quite considerable to those who live with and around the addict. There is a huge need for family assistance, programmes and support. This process will usually be introduced in rehab. Family members will be introduced to Al-Anon and other support groups which are specifically for their needs. Yet the business of rehab is to enable recovery to begin for the addicted person who wishes to change.

A medically assisted detox, in some cases to remove the substances from the body in a safe way, or a period where the using behaviour is halted – Abstinence.

Therapy – to examine the thinking, feelings and behaviour and effect a change in all these areas. This is a big challenge. Lengths of stay in a rehab vary from seven days to a few months. The job of changing thinking, feelings and behaviour is actually a lifelong job so, however long someone is able to stay in treatment, is never long enough to finish the job. However long it is, it is just the start. Many people who have successfully started their recovery in a rehab talk about the "protective bubble", which is true. The addict is protected from the outside world and self, whilst learning the basics of recovery. The outside world retreats, whilst the addict gains enough sense of self to ask and answer questions about what has been going on in their lives. If they can see it, accept that using will no longer help, and work with others to find the answer to the changes needed, this is the **start** of recovery. Unfortunately, many, including the addict, think that at this point they are better now. There are many problems and pitfalls up ahead in order to recover, and **communication and connection** are the components needed to succeed. It is these that the addict needs to find in these early days. Addicts crave solitude and secrecy, and they need to learn to be with and communicate honestly with others.

Dual Diagnosis

Dual Diagnosis complicates an already complicated diagnosis and benefits from treatment in a rehab as opposed to just going to an Anonymous meeting.

The term dual diagnosis is a term used by the medical profession. It is used to describe a situation where other serious illnesses develop or exist alongside the addiction. Things such as depression and anxiety are common in addiction. Not so common but equally devastating are things like bi-polar illness, personality disorders and many more. What they all have in common is that the addicts who have these additional mental health issues may have used substances as a way of coping with them. What needs to be understood is that both or all disorders need to be treated. For instance, many addicts are profoundly depressed when they reach treatment; many have believed that if the depression goes away through treatment or prescribed medication, then all will be well. There are many who have taken anti-depressants for years and/or had counselling with no cessation of symptoms, simply because continuing to drink alcohol or using mind-altering substances to feel better will sabotage any progress. When individuals are diagnosed, both or all illnesses need attention. There have been many relapses when one or the other serious mental health issue has not been addressed correctly, or missed altogether, because it is assumed by the addict and everyone concerned that if only the using would stop all would be well.

Recovery from addiction is difficult and relapses are common. There is a huge fear in some that the taking of prescribed medication will escalate the addiction. Certainly in the early days of treatment it was believed that patients should be taken off all medications at once to "see" what would be left. This could be very dangerous practice for some, and certainly for some individuals, this was cruel and unnecessary. This decision should be left in the hands of the medical teams who understand addiction. Of course, there are the old stories of addicts who have manipulated doctors and their medications and no doubt this will continue, but as science and medicine improve, perhaps old attitudes and behaviours can also improve.

Chapter 9
Communication and Connection

Two of the most important concepts to acquire. It seems absurd perhaps that grown-ups, some who have families, have businesses and in many ways seem to be leading successful lives, have to learn how to communicate. Yet the disease relies on denial, on half-truths and lies; the addict, as the disease develops, becomes better and better at concealing the truth. This denial serves to blind the addict as to what is actually going on. In some cases, coming into rehab and being encouraged to examine what has been going on is a huge shock. Most addicts in these initial stages go through massive amounts of shame, guilt and self-loathing. If statistics of successful suicide where alcohol and drugs are implicated are to be believed, then this is a dangerous time for the addict. Another reason why rehab is a good idea in some cases. Talking about behaviours honestly with others, and putting together the history and seeing the progression of what's been happening is hard. The disease concept gives an explanation as to unfathomable behaviour. However, it is not a "get out of jail free" clause. It is not an excuse to carry on because they can't help it. Because with the knowledge of the disease also comes the knowledge that there are ways to manage it. It will be in these fragile early days that the information is introduced that the problem is not the substance or addictive behaviour, but that **I AM THE PROBLEM. My thinking is flawed.**

Who or what am I? A profound question of course, many books written, many theories told, and fabulous minds engaged in this question; so we will not get too complicated with this question. The addict should be encouraged and supported when questioning who or what they are, and when examining the problems they have with addictive behaviour. By the time rehab is suggested as a solution, the behaviours have most likely become entrenched and horrendous. Many addicts enter treatment believing they are despicable human beings. The shame and remorse are strong, and once the denial ceases, this feeling escalates. Self-esteem will be at an all-time low. Good treatment will recognise this fact and work with the addict to change this. Learning that good people sometimes can do bad things can be very cathartic for some. Learning that in order to make amends they have to stop the behaviour is also another crucial moment. "Sorry", will no longer work, however, "sorry" plus a change in behaviour is different.

Human beings mostly do things because they think it will be good for them. Few people engage in behaviour because they think it will be bad for them. So in the case of addiction, the addict has learnt that to use benefits them. The use of the substance gives a feeling that is translated as good, the feeling is one of being at ease, comfort or euphoria. Most addicts do not use to feel bad, or do bad things. The fact that bad things happen more and more as the disease progresses is because the addict simply does not see it, or the addict is enmeshed in a belief system that says that this time I will/can control it. They are enmeshed in a system that uses to feel better despite the adverse consequences, and the fact that control is unpredictable. They are enmeshed in **insane thinking.** The way they think is the problem, and the neural pathways of the addict's brain are wired to translate want to need. The addict needs to use in order to feel better. **They think this, they think this, they think this.** Without help, they cannot think differently. They do not know this is happening, they cannot see it, and nor does anyone else. It is usually only recognised when the disease has progressed sufficiently to show adverse behaviour. Research now does recognise the genetic aspect of addiction and blood tests can pick up genetic markers that will predict a problem. But, as always, these test are expensive and not readily available. So until they are, education is the best resource. Communication is how I access this information and make it personal to me. Discussion, debate, questions and answers are the best way to learn. If I experience this through connection to another, it makes it more powerful, a book is brilliant, the Internet amazing, but you and I talking about things that baffle many is always going to be the best way to learn.

Before walking into my first meeting, I had discussed staying sober endlessly with family and friends. I had made promises that I meant but could never keep. I had changed jobs for instance and had stopped working at sea as the party lifestyle was the problem. I changed countries as maybe that would do it. I read about alcohol and drug problems, I identified with the people who played these tortured characters in movies and in books. I could never remain sober or clean, no matter how much I wanted to, how much I willed it because there was always another situation/person/incident that made sobriety and being clean impossible. I thought I must be mad. I thought I was a terrible person. I hated hurting the people I loved, but I couldn't stop until I went to a meeting, and learnt how not to pick up one day at a time. I learnt this from another person in recovery. It made no sense at first, but I learnt that by not drinking or using addictive substances, I could halt a disease that was wrecking my life. I was shocked to learn I had an illness, even doubting it could be as serious as this sounded. I was shocked, but also I was ashamed, I would have given anything for what ailed me to be called something else, "a depression, perhaps". I sometimes despair at the ignorance of my younger self, as I know now, depression, often accompanied by addiction, is an equally devastating illness, but perhaps in my defence, I felt back then it would be more acceptable. I was shocked by many things I learned in the meetings. But shocking though some of this education was, the incredible thing is that I learnt how to stay clean and sober. I was such a fearful soul in those early days. I am eternally grateful to the many people who befriended, helped and supported me. It was they who first connected with me, and it was they who taught me how to communicate. It was this that helped me find recovery and stay in recovery. This way of communicating and connecting and helping the addict continues to this day. It is what makes the Anonymous movement unique and effective.

Chapter 10
The Disease Concept

Addiction is a chronic disease that is progressive, has no cure and is fatal. If the true nature of addiction is not worked on, then the addict, and everyone else, can be lulled into a false sense of security when the using stops. Be it a substance and/ or behaviour. Of course some of the serious life problems seem to dissipate when the using stops, the body repairs itself, relationships improve, etc. and life feels better. However, if the addict does not continue to stay focused, change and grow, then old behaviours, patterns of thinking and feelings will return. Most addicted people believe that once the substance or addictive behaviour ceases, then so will the problems. Not so, as already discussed in previous chapters. This is only the beginning. There are many books and articles written on this subject which will be referenced later on. Addicts should educate themselves, do the research, read the books. The problem is one of flawed thinking. The addict has a mind that believes it is a good thing to take a drink or drug despite evidence built up over years that should convince otherwise. In order to recover and stay in recovery, addicts will need to develop new ways of handling the way they think and feel. If they don't, they can be viewed as "dry drunk"; this is a derogatory term used to describe the behaviours and actions of people who have stopped using but to all intents and purposes are no better/nicer/pleasant to be around than when they were using. Some friends or relatives of a dry drunk have been known to wish the user would resume the addiction as their "sober" behaviour is so unpleasant. The behaviour eventually becomes painful to the addict; if they see the effect on others, this makes it worse and if nothing intervenes, then to resume the using will be the solution. Ways to change are learnt in the Anonymous Meetings or through therapy, (or both). Understanding of this concept should go a long way to "prove" that this disease is more to do with the thinking behind behaviours. The feelings and actions of someone who is in recovery are vastly different from that of someone who has just stopped using. Many times husbands, wives or friends of someone who has just stopped using and done nothing else, will complain that nothing seems to have changed. The person is still angry or unpleasant or acting in ways that cause concern. From time to time, there have been utterances of "*I wish he/she would just have a drink. They were nicer to be around when they were drinking.*" A sad statement perhaps, but it does illustrate that changes made by working a programme of recovery have to happen. Sobriety is a state of mind rather than absence of a substance or the using behaviour. The programme of recovery has to be kept firmly to the forefront of consciousness, otherwise the addiction has the capacity to return to its destructive state. Accepting addiction as a disease cannot possibly be seen as a "cop out" when the individuals with it have to work so hard for it to remain in its passive phase. They have to continue the work always, no days off. This is a disease for life. How can this be known as a "cop-out?"

Chapter 11
Anger

Anger, when associated with addiction, is almost always destructive and out of control. Anger and resentment seem to latch onto addicts; resentment is a major cause of relapse. Addicts don't know how to handle many of their feelings. Anger is one of the most destructive. To continue to recover, addicts have to learn how to handle this feeling differently. It is part of life, of course, to feel stressed and angry. To indulge it or ignore it is to invite problems, especially for the newly recovering addict. It continues to grow and becomes more and more problematic, unless dealt with correctly. Rage and anger are often a feature of early recovery. As the individual sobers up, it can be very disconcerting to be, or indeed, perplexing to live alongside someone who is acting like a stroppy teenager. Fine and understandable perhaps in teenagers, not so in the supposedly "sober" individual who is desperate to be seen to be changing and coming across in a better light. The newly sober/clean individual has a lot of growing up to do. It is said that the emotional life of an addict stops developing adequately from the start of their addictive using. True or not, an inability to handle anger will easily derail any recovery, so help with this feeling in particular must be found. This can be achieved with the more experienced members of Alcoholics Anonymous or through Therapists who specialise in addiction. The programme of recovery includes examining life histories, not as is sometimes thought, to blame an event or person for the addiction, but for the addicted person to examine and find their role in every situation. Addicts are essentially selfish and self-seeking, especially in the throes of the illness. But this attitude does not just disappear in recovery; early recovery seems to be littered with events which end up with the recovering person getting angry and harbouring resentments and grudges to the world at large! Bill Wilson, the founder of AA, wrote, that "resentment is the number one offender, destroying more alcoholics than anything else." He also said, "our liquor was but a symptom". Discovering self is what the 12 Step programme can be described as doing. The addict's most compelling job is to change. Once the alcohol, drugs etc. have been removed, the addict is left with a self they don't know or understand. The people in the addict's world also do not understand them; the behaviour when using has been so unreasonable and out of control it is not unusual for everyone to feel huge amounts of anger. If this were to continue, the addict would, of course, revert back to the thing that makes life bearable, the addiction, and so the terrible journey continues until madness, illness or death stops this progression. The 12 Step programme addresses some of the anger, but in some cases this is not enough and counselling/therapy should also be an option. There are many types of therapies and therapists and many Anger Management Courses available, which are of immeasurable benefit. However, it is essential for everyone to remember that for the addict the quickest most effective solution to pain and problems is to use. This way of fixing the feelings is ingrained and very seductive. Other ways of changing feelings have to be found and become also ingrained.

Chapter 12
Sleeping Tiger

Addiction is sometimes described as a sleeping tiger. That once recovery through abstinence has been achieved, then the disease must be kept in its dormant stage. As addicts learn to negotiate life on life's terms, they are advised to stay away from risky people and risky places. That socialising with people who still use, going to parties, clubs and "wet" places can almost certainly wake up that sleeping tiger. As can many other things. Things that on the surface could be perceived as good things to do, like holidays for instance, may end up creating more stress than is good for the addict. Christmas, weddings and holidays are all potentially difficult in the early days. It will not always be so, of course, and the recovering person will learn fast, but if he/she is smart, they will learn that most life-changing events should be negotiated and planned with the help of others. Learning how to live again must be done with the help of others; trying to fly solo will result in crashes, relapses, failure. In early recovery there are many "firsts". Things that have been done many times in someone's life can become quite difficult to negotiate in recovery. Things feel new, different, and sometimes impossible. Keeping the tiger slumbering is a skill. It is not a skill that is achievable alone. It is the responsibility of the recovering person to ensure that their emotional and mental health is good. To become aware that in times of high emotional stress which life seems to dole out quite randomly, they need to take care and ensure feelings are kept in a manageable state. This is achieved through communication, by stepping up meetings, finding a therapist to do extra work. Whatever it takes really to quiet the emotions and mind. This is difficult to do at first. Most human beings are taught it is good to be self-sufficient, but for the addict, this can be a disaster. If they can learn early on in recovery to use the experience of others as a template, they will save themselves a lot of heartache. When an individual goes to meetings of the Anonymous fellowship, they are introduced to the 12 Steps. These, simply put, are a route, a way of staying sober and clean using certain methods which the newcomer is encouraged to adopt by listening and following the directions of more established members. The Steps are simple to understand, but perhaps difficult to put into action in life. Many addicts fail to sustain recovery due to the concept of "handing the will over", which is discussed in Step 3 of the 12 Steps. It is perhaps the most difficult to understand and to continue to adhere to. Addicts are often described as self-will run riot; addicts are sometimes described as stubborn, which they can certainly be, but the self-will that is described in recovery circles is much more than stubbornness. It has elements of arrogance, anger and ego which the addict has to learn to let go of. It is this egotistical element that will that often causes so many issues for people in recovery. *"I want what I want when I want it."* Selfishness beyond reason. If the addict can begin to understand that the disease is a problem of flawed thinking, then perhaps letting go would be easier. Addicts have to begin to understand that in times of high stress, the thinking process can be compromised. If they begin their recovery by understanding this one fact, then finding solutions by seeking and accepting help/support from others will be no big deal. "Handing over the will", which is one of the concepts of AA, is often seen as difficult, or translated as becoming a doormat or unable to make decisions. This is so far from the truth; however, in order to stay well, the newly recovering person needs to remember they have flawed thinking, which if left to their own devices, will get them into trouble. Handing over simply means talking about plans, especially life-changing ones, in order to make better decisions. In times of stress, the addict's ability to handle emotions and difficult issues can become quite compromised. Recovery means seeking help from others at these times. This process shows that addiction and recovery are not the simple "just say no" idea that is often thought. It requires humility, hard work and persistence. Remember that the drinking or using in an addictive way is just a symptom of what is really wrong with the addict. Once the destructive part of addiction has been stopped and abstinence achieved, the real work of recovery can then start. If this is not understood then, yet again the idea that the addict is fixed will come back, the need for persistence and help to change will be lost, and the merry go round starts up again. Keeping the tiger slumbering is a difficult job. But if remembered, it will save much trouble in early recovery. It will also perhaps save lives, as getting back into recovery after relapse is almost harder than at the start. Shame, despair and futility seem to follow relapses around. Being in this mental state is dangerous, of course, but so is all the damage to mind body and soul that occurs when relapse happens. There are never any winners with relapse. It is always miserable and sometimes it is fatal.

Chapter 13
The God Stuff

So, if the addicts' thinking is flawed, how are they to proceed? In the Anonymous Meetings the concept of a Higher Power is introduced. Because there is so much resistance to the simple little word 'God', treatment centres and others have attempted to translate this into a more workable concept, with no disrespect intended to any religion or to the founders of AA who were men of their times – raised in the Bible belt area of Middle America. Of course, the language of the literature and the fellowship that followed sounds the way it does. But the literature does stress that the Higher Power is to be "as understood by the individual," treatment centres who use these concepts sometimes talk about the Higher Power as "the individual, plus others." The others, of course, should have some understanding of addiction and recovery, otherwise it would be easy to be steered in wrong directions. Even if someone starts this journey with a belief in a religious God, the concept of working with others is one that will succeed. The simple truth is that Anonymous meetings work on all levels. There has been much misinformation and misunderstanding about them. This sadly has cost some their lives. There are many wonderful stories in the recovery world of how people found their own particular "miracle". Stories of how from places of desperation and despair an individual has been able to turn their life around and be different. Some will say they don't really know what happened, but something did and now it is different. Does it come from God, or the universe, or from the desire of the individual, who knows? Does it matter? Surely what matters is that for millions in the world today, after plugging into the help available from a 12 Step meeting, they are different and are no longer behaving in a way that is destructive and dangerous.

After my last drunk and having decided to give AA a try, I stood outside in the street contemplating the people walking in. From my lofty position of nursing a black eye and a hangover, I intended to make sure that the people walking in were "Okay". What clinched it for me was the arrival of a man on a motorbike, who parked and walked in. I thought he looked cool and, therefore, felt it would be all right to follow him into the meeting. Always someone who liked signs and omens, my befuddled mind chose to believe it was a message from my brother who had been killed way too young, two years previously on his motorbike. Much of the meeting was and is a blur in my memory; I never saw the motorbike guy again, but I do remember individuals telling me that I did not have to drink. Revolutionary! Although it sounds ludicrous to me now, I had only ever tried to limit my blackouts by drinking less, the idea of not drinking at all was news to me! I heard it was the first drink that did the damage, that one meeting was not enough, that I was sick, not bad, and endless things that clarified what I had been doing to myself and my life. Although this does not in any way

71

sound miraculous, what else explains the fact that from this experience thirty plus years ago to now, I have never picked up a mood-altering substance again. I had some issues with "The God Stuff" in the early days, but was so desperate for help I chose to listen to the older wiser members of the groups who told me it would all sort itself out. That the important thing initially was to stop drinking and using. All I needed to achieve this was an open mind, and to follow some simple rules. It was in the following of the rules that sobriety was achieved. I like to believe today that it really was a sign from my brother, and my sobriety today is my way of honouring his memory and saying thank you.

More God Stuff

Because this is such an important sticking point in people getting help, and to explore what the God Stuff really means to individuals who have found recovery, I have asked several people with varying ideas of what it means to them to contribute their thoughts. They will be identified by first name alone as is the custom in AA.

1   The God Thing

The God Thing kept me from AA for six years, and those were not pleasant years; six years of trying everything but AA to deal with my alcoholism. Years of continual failure and frustration. As I look back at these years, the problem was/is simple, I am a devout and daily practicing atheist, and AA is rather full of religious language. When I was serious about doing something about my problem, I received three pieces of advice which were:

Don't worry about the small stuff – There is a famous saying in my own line of work that fits well. "It is inappropriate to be concerned about mice when there are tigers abroad." If alcoholism is dismantling your life, worrying about religious beliefs needs to be at the bottom of the list. When you understand the concepts of AA better, you learn that in some of the literature it states that AA must never compel anyone to pay, believe or conform to anything, to do so may condemn the alcoholic who is looking for help to a life of endless misery. Go to a meeting and see – try several before deciding, there are many and all are different. You will meet people for whom the meetings are working. You are advised to not write off things before investigation. Having very thoroughly proved to myself that my way of dealing with alcoholism didn't work, I should have been a lot quicker in trying a method that does work for an enormous number of people. Ignoring the evidence of my own experience kept me from recovery. Accepting the evidence of my own experience and of the people I met at AA moved me into recovery.

Take what is useful and leave the rest – I have learnt to give everything a fair hearing. The meetings contain an extremely diverse group of people; it should be no surprise that there are a huge variety of ideas, opinions and experiences expressed by its members. The AA phrase "look for the similarities and not the differences" is useful to remember. It is also useful to remember that AA offers a planned, staged programme of recovery, and that it does not offer a pick and mix, quick-fix recovery. In other words, I follow the full suggested programme and do not skip the bits I don't like. As I write this now, the thing that worries me is that all this appears to be too simple. However, this is just a case of my poor old brain trying to compare my previous existence as an active alcoholic with my current life as a recovering alcoholic

Brian : Sobriety date: November 2010

2   Higher Power

You would have thought that as a Christian writing about my Higher Power would be easy, but it's not. Firstly, because my faith disappeared in active addiction and secondly, because my beliefs, although they are in the same God, are somehow different. I ran away from God because life was not doing what I wanted life to do. I thought I believed in a kind, all powerful, forgiving God who had my best interest at heart. The trouble was I didn't trust my God at all. Alcoholism brought me to a place of hopelessness, a place without faith because my way wasn't working. A different way of believing started when I got sober and went to AA. I returned to an understanding that God loves me the way I am.

I got my choice back through following the AA program, the listening to and acting on the principles of the people in recovery around me. I believe we are not meant to live in isolation, but are meant to use the help of others. My belief is contained in the Martin Luther King saying: "I sought my soul. But my soul I could not see. I sought my God. But my God eluded me. I sought my brother and I found all three."

3 *Higher Power*

When I first encountered the words Higher Power in relation to my recovery, I thought, "no problem". I had my own belief system which stemmed from ten years of convent education, and, whilst not a Catholic, I adored the extravagant and exotic Latin services, never missing a chance to enter this world. I had parents who sent me to Sunday school, which led to a place in the choir, bell ringing and later assisting with the church youth club. I thought I had a hot line to God more refined than most.

I was to find this thinking was part of the grandiosity I displayed. There was no hotline. I merely provided my own answers. Being so advanced or special and different, as AA calls it. Did not of course need an AA sponsor to guide or question me.

After relapsing twice, I began to understand something had to change. I began to listen and to ask questions, tentatively at first, as the realisation that I knew nothing grated and my pride proved a stubborn obstacle.

When I was admitted into treatment for the third time, I would have stood on my head at midnight and brayed at the moon if it would help. I was ready to listen and to think. I was lucky to have a patient counsellor who suggested using my peers initially as a "Higher Power", explaining that I could always use the analogy of segments of an orange to make up the whole, if I found it difficult to trust my peers alone. I began adding other powerful and positive phenomena, a sponsor, a new friend in recovery to form my collective "Higher Power".

Slowly, I came to accept this power needed to be something outside of myself, something more important than me. Something honest and marvellous, with my best interests the priority, even if I baulked at the responses I received at times. This was truly a struggle. Being asked to "hand over my life and my self-will" felt like doctrine. It felt like a loss of freedom until I fully understood it was giving me freedom from my twisted thinking, it was giving me the freedom to become the person I wanted to be.

I still struggle with self-will and forget at times to be grateful, but my life is now focused on something far bigger and far more important than just myself these days. I am not sure how it happened, but I know that something, or someone looks out for me, intervenes when I need help and has given me purpose and self-respect.

Elizabeth: Sobriety date 2nd July 1992

4   Higher Power thoughts

There is nothing very spiritual about the way I view the Higher Power aspect of my recovery, certainly not religious. It is not one thing, but many. It is anything that can help me with the task or trouble at hand. It could simply be the instruction manual for a new electronic device. For a more serious matter it would be a doctor in a medical emergency. The world is a vast catalogue of people who can help, machines that can perform tasks and tools that can be used to put things back together when they break. The thing to remember is that there is always something, or someone that can help, if I remember to look outside of myself.

By myself I only have a limited amount of knowledge, energy or power to deal with an infinite variety of life's challenges. It is not a fault, it is the same for all of us. Asking for help and seeking guidance will always give me a greater power to deal with whatever life throws my way. In simple terms, if I want to hammer nails, I need a hammer. Without the hammer it's gonna take a long time and be pretty painful. Me, plus the hammer, is a Power Greater than myself.

Mark : Sobriety date: 4th February 2010

5 Recovery

The first spiritual word that I encountered in recovery was WE – the beginning of relief from the bondage of self. Sometime later I told a member of our fellowship that I was choosing nature as my Higher Power. His response was, "What is the most natural thing for an alcoholic to do?"

"Drink," I said.

"Then you are going to need something supernatural to stay sober." Thus began my spiritual journey. I actively sought and asked my Higher Power to show me how and where; I then found intellectual sense, inner peace, joy and love. I converted to Catholicism. It has strengthened my sobriety. From being a broken, abused abuser, I am now thirty-three years sober with peace of mind and serenity. Healed of all that was done to me and all I have done to others.

Recovery, for me, has not been about being strong, but about accepting my countless weaknesses and turning to my Higher Power who does for me what I cannot do for myself.

Angie: Sobriety date: 9th February 1981

6   Thoughts about Higher Power

I arrived at a meeting of Alcoholics Anonymous thinking that the worst thing in the world had happened. I, a chronic alcoholic, who had lost everything including all self-respect, really thought that I could sink no lower than to have to endure the ignominy of having to attend meetings with men in dirty macs who slept on park benches. At my first meeting I saw slogans which included the word God. They are quite nice welcoming people, I thought, but do not have my worries, so do not understand, and I want nothing to do with this God business at all. As an only child from a secular family, I attended a Convent for twelve years; I was not a Catholic, so was labelled a non-Catholic and segregated during religious ceremonies. I came to perceive that God was punishing. The order of nuns was a closed order that had very little dealings with the outside world. I was not a meek child and the thought of being condemned to eternal damnation provoked the response that I may as well be killed for a sheep than a lamb, so I rebelled and am afraid did my worst.

In AA I was asked, not told, to follow a spiritual rather than religious programme for living, in order to help me stop drinking. Although I was extremely sceptical to say the least, I had nowhere else to go, having burned all my boats through my alcoholic behaviour. The people in AA were the only people who welcomed me.

What I discovered was a way of life that was interesting, fascinating, and sometimes painful when changes had to be made in order to stay sober. During these painful times when I despaired and disliked myself intensely and felt I could not succeed, I was asked to try to rely on what was termed a Higher Power. It was explained to me that as an alcoholic, I had no power whatsoever over my alcoholic drinking, and was asked to try to find a power greater than myself to help. At first I found this was the AA meetings, as the members were people who had succeeded in stopping, and their collective power was certainly greater than any power I could muster alone. In time, the group was succeeded by a power termed a God of my understanding. It was not the power of a vengeful God that I chose, but one whose love and compassion had the ability to help me and many others overcome their alcohol problems.

These days I recognise the power in asking for help, the power in giving help and the power in sobriety where I am not a slave to craving. This power, this God of my understanding, has helped me stay sober and happy for thirty-five years. I have a life far beyond anything I could have imagined. I have peace of mind, friends, and a loving partner. I travel, have hobbies and my life is full and interesting. I am so grateful to have found my Higher Power.

Olivia: Sobriety date: November 1979

As these stories show, this "God stuff" and what it means to people is varied and different. There are religious and non-religious people who have got well using the 12 Step Anonymous meetings. Why should a tiny little three-letter word cause so many problems? The truth is it does not have to, but it will for all those looking for an excuse, or to prove that the meetings cannot possibly work for them. Try them, stay around for longer than one meeting, engage in conversation, talk to people, and ask for help. You may be amazed at what happens and it is amazing what happens to and for some individuals.

To recover from an addictive illness, individuals need to recognize and accept that there is a problem. The problem is not other people, places or things. Once the problem is discovered and is accepted, they then need to accept they cannot rectify this problem alone. If they could, they would already have done so. Other recovering addicts and alcoholics will tell them they need to stop using and stay stopped. The power of others working to give the suffering alcoholic information, guidance and support enables abstinence to occur and endure. It is the power of collective thinking, strength and will. Some of them may be religious, some will be atheist, some will be Buddhists, or whatever. It doesn't actually matter what we want to call any of this. Call it something or nothing, the power of the collective force is what helps.

Chapter 14
Families, Friends and Significant Others

This heading has not been left until late because it is unimportant, it is perhaps one of the most important to consider in recovery. A book about addiction naturally focuses on the addict, however if family, friends and loved ones are not considered, there is really no point. What happens to spouses, partners, parents, children and other family members is equally devastating in the progression of this illness. More relationships come to untimely ends because the issue is not addressed. It is yet another manifestation of the misunderstanding about the disease concept. When the addiction is in free fall, people rarely talk about what is happening. Because denial is present and deception has become the name of the game, partners often end up running out of things to say and do, the threats, the pleas, the ultimatums have all been fruitless. It is not uncommon for spouses or partners or others to believe that they are mad themselves, they are often left with a huge feeling of hopelessness and rage that by the time they or the addict seeks help, it is often too late for the relationship. Or because so much emphasis is placed on the addict, it is not uncommon for family members to feel "What about me?" If a recovery is to be successful and for relationships to survive, then time needs to be spent in helping family members and everyone come to terms with this illness themselves. They have sometimes been unwilling participants in the downward spiral of the addiction, often becoming ill themselves. Interestingly, it is this aspect of addiction that family members and others have the biggest problem with; they too mistake the taking of the substance as the only manifestation of the illness, when, as already discussed, it is more to do with attitudes, feelings and behaviours. Family members/others have these too, of course, and in the progression of the addict's illness, they have been adapting and changing sometimes in unhealthy ways in order to cope with the situation. Most rehabs will introduce family members to support groups and effect introductions to the outside helping agencies such as Al-Anon or Co-dependants Anonymous, who have long known that a successful recovery will need to include help for families as well as any significant others in the addicts life.

In the case of children, many addicted parents who come into treatment want to believe that they have hidden their behaviour and problems from their children. This is not the case as anyone who has worked with addicts and their families will testify. Children are pretty astute, they will notice most things that are happening in the family; they may not translate what is going on into coherent scripts, but they certainly notice. They themselves can be adversely affected by issues in the family. The solution as always is communication and connection. To ignore this aspect of the problem is a huge mistake. Conversations with children can be started with the help of therapists if need be, and children can go for therapy themselves; there is an organisation for teenagers named Al-Ateen. Younger children blossom when things are explained and they are listened to. There are many ways to begin the communication. The important message is that it should begin. To not do this leaves all family members open to problems in the future. If the anger and the feelings of helplessness are not addressed and worked on, the relationships become strained. Strain in relationships is another reason relapses are common in early recovery. Unexpressed feelings of rage and anger can develop into stress and depression, and with all these elements in the mix, the insanity of addiction claims more lives and destruction.

It is often not enough just for the addict to receive treatment. Many, many partners, children and loved ones are going through hell because their feelings are not being addressed. It is fairly common for everyone to believe that the problems in family life only lies with the persons drinking or using. The problems with partners or children may go unnoticed and emerge sometimes months or years later. Partners end up leaving the addict and find that their next relationships are equally problematic because the patterns of adapting and coping with addiction have not been addressed. There may be other illnesses and problems, such as depression, stress, anxiety or sleeplessness; the list goes on and on. Children, of course are the next generation who have potential problems with addiction. Un-expressed emotions, confusing lives, people at war, all culminating to produce the perfect breeding ground for addiction. Genetics play their part, but there is also the need for certain elements to be present for addiction to manifest itself. Residues of the traumatic family life that are experienced are some of these other things.

For friends of people with addictions this is also a difficult area to address in the beginning. Addicts are advised to stay away from risky places and influences, especially in the first few months of a recovery. It is difficult for everyone when the things that used to be done and the places that used to be frequented suddenly need to stop. Genuine friendships, however, endure the changes. Once again, if the seriousness of the addict's plight is understood by the addict first and foremost, then explaining to friends is not so difficult. The addict, however, sometimes goes to extraordinary lengths to appear "normal." Statements such as "Why should others have to go without a drink because of me" or "go ahead, I don't mind," are often uttered by newly recovering people. People with a more robust recovery will explain that if one had a peanut allergy, would we be so cavalier about it? Of course not, peanut allergies are taken very seriously, with food labelled, and the stuff avoided at all costs for fear of what may occur. Addiction to drugs and alcohol hold the same dangers for some people. Many things influence human beings, and taking care around and being aware of those influences should become second nature if one is serious about staying well.

There are so many changes that need to take place in a recovering person's life. So many events which need to be avoided, especially in the early days or planned carefully to minimise the dangers. If this is not understood and done, then massive risks are taken with fragile recoveries. If it is not explained to family members, they can often feel resentful about yet more restrictions placed on them and life. Yet as and when adjustments to lifestyles are made and family relationships improved, any restrictions will be viewed as well worth it. It all, however, takes time and much discussion.

"Intervention" written by Bill Stevens

Misery, fear, frustration, hopelessness, these are just some of the repeated feelings experienced by the families when untreated addiction is in full flow, or even when just in its developing stage. Intervention brings about the opportunity for treatment and recovery, sooner rather than later. Family interventions developed after it became apparent that coerced treatment can be just as successful a route for recovery as voluntary referrals. It was observed that American courts would and could mandate residential treatment at the point of sentencing. These less than ready or willing people proved that specialist treatment works, regardless of initial motivation to enter a programme. Outcome studies were on a par for the self-referred and the mandated clients from courts. This put paid to the belief that "you cannot help an alcoholic until they want help". If the courts can do this, could Treatment Specialists replicate this in the family, or workplace? So Family Intervention began and the results continue to be startling. A Family Intervention requires planning and attention to detail along with a willingness of all concerned to put aside old ideas, fears and reservations. A huge percentage of phone calls for help with addiction problems come from "concerned others". The Interventionist is a specialist addictions therapist who has experience in all aspects of family structure, of addiction and is aware of treatment services available that will match the person's clinical needs. They are normally independent of any treatment provider and will have membership of the Association of Intervention Specialists. This ensures standards are high as they lead people through this experience.

More information about Intervention and Bill Stevens are to be found in the reference section of this book.

Chapter 15
Anonymous Meetings versus Therapy AGAIN

So which is best? They are both worthwhile, of course, and neither can be said to be better than the other. At the start of someone's recovery perhaps a spell in a rehab will be needed if the disease is well advanced or meetings have been tried with no success. It is hard to walk into an AA meeting for instance and to be able to understand how it all works; many do it, and how brilliant is that? But some cannot get recovery this way. So if that is the case, Rehab or counselling is an answer. However, any rehab worth its salt will be advising that Anonymous meetings are a must after treatment. Very often, they will be introduced, explained and demystified as part of treatment. Individual therapy may be needed as well at any time. When life throws some of its more difficult things at people, then extra therapy may be needed to get through. The meetings and therapy are ways of staying focused, and of processing difficult issues and of managing feelings. However, some issues will always need professional help. Anonymous meetings are in the business of keeping people clean/sober and focused. It cannot act as marriage guidance or relationship mediator, although many marriages and relationships improve when the using stops some problems need extra help. The meetings do not deal with financial issues or grief counselling and so on. The meetings do many things for many people, but sometimes professional counselling should be sought. But as an addition to the Anonymous programme, not, instead of.

Much information exists for people interested in educating themselves further about Alcoholics Anonymous, but very simply it was started over seventy years ago by two men who found a way to stay sober. The 12 Steps are a set of simple instructions of how they managed to do this, and today these Steps are the principles and concepts that recovering addicts use to stay sober. As already discussed the language of the time makes them sound old fashioned, or like religious dogma, but this first impression is usually dispelled if the addict can stick around meetings long enough. Alcoholism was the first addiction to benefit from using the 12 Steps, but over the years they have been adapted to enable many more of the addictive problems to be addressed this way. The Steps need to be understood and incorporated into life, and they offer a progressive way of how to remain abstinent, of how to change, of how to make amends for terrible behaviour, and ultimately how to find purpose and reason in life. Bill W., the founder of AA, has been quoted as saying "selfishness is at the root of our problems". The 12 Steps offer a way to work on, to look at, understand and change self on a deep and personal level. In an abstinence-based Rehab setting, if the Steps are used, then the first three Steps are usually the ones concentrated on. Step 1 is about Surrender, admittance and acceptance. Step 2 is about believing help is needed, and Step 3 is the action step, what is needed to get and accept help. These

Steps are not concentrated on because the others are not important, but because if the concept of the first three Steps are achieved, then an individual will buy themselves enough time to begin the process of recovery. If the individual has reached Step 3 in a treatment setting, they will also have been introduced to other recovering people and the meetings. If the individual has accepted the programme so far, they will know that on-going meetings and continued work on self is necessary.

There are many types of recovery meetings. There are meetings in every city of Britain, sometimes more than one. They can be found in many countries of the world. It is worth while investigating. In the last few pages of the Big Book there is a quote attributed to Herbert Spencer which states, "There is a principal which is a bar against all information, which is proof against all arguments and which cannot fail to keep a man in everlasting ignorance – that principal is contempt prior to investigation".

Yet sadly, contempt for this method of recovery is often voiced by intelligent people. The number of relapses that happen even when addicts access the Anonymous Meetings or Rehab is seen as the reason it is not an effective. Many, including the addicts themselves, misunderstand, misidentify and treat the addiction incorrectly. Until there is a change in how information about this disease is disseminated, then needless misery and destruction will continue to dominate.

The good work that is done in many Anonymous meetings around the country and around the world should be celebrated so that people are not ashamed to go to them. The great work done in the many abstinence-based rehabs in this country and around the world should be acknowledged. Funding for treatment should be more easily available. Programmes for the children of addicts and for the families of addicts should gain prominence. There are many amazing workers in this field who just quietly get on with the job in hand, and there are many people in recovery who have years and years of experience and give their time freely. All of these things are the positive aspects of the recovery world. Yet insanely, what are the things which dominate media and people's consciousness?

The failures of rehabilitation.
The well-known people in the media, who relapse spectacularly.
The wasted youth, dying whilst experimenting with yet more new drugs.
The suicide statistics.
The criminality associated with addiction.
The drug barons making millions selling their wares.
The failure of the drug laws.
The prisons, the institutions, the hospitals all struggling to cope with the epidemic.

So I return to the statement made at the beginning, what do I hope will be achieved with this book? Something needs to change in our world, and the twisted, twisted way in which addiction is sometimes perceived, can and must change. We need to educate, and we need to make treatment available and accessible. We need to break free from the coils of these twisted wires. For some, the release from addiction never comes. Addicts die in many ways. Perhaps the saddest deaths are the ones who die by their own hands. One of the statistics about suicide is that in many successful attempts, alcohol or other drugs are present.

Moriatta Falls

She chose this place from thousands she
Had access to.
It was said, she googled it
Made it real,
And went to see.
She chose this place, maybe
Like me, she thought it
Sounded beautiful.
It sounded peaceful, or even spectacular -
So she went to see,
Thought it fit –
Didn't think –
Held her breath and jumped.

Moriatta Falls was written in 2008 after I received the news that the young daughter of a friend of mine had killed herself. She had struggled within the coils of her illness for years, and everything she and her family tried had not brought solution. She was loved and came from a loving family. The shock, sadness and rage I discovered within myself after hearing the news has stayed with me. It was her suicide that prompted me to think about the twisted thinking that occurs in some. The tragedies, the waste, the ugliness and the hopeless, helpless feelings that surround addicts and addiction.

Many who work in the field of addiction know these feelings; we all hope the work we do with addicts and their families can make a difference. For some, the help comes too late, or the message does not penetrate the muddled thinking; it can feel like a hopeless and endless task at times, so why do we keep trying? The answer, of course, is because in the story of addiction, twisted wires, broken lives, death and pain, there lies another truth. The flip side of the dark is light, and recovery is possible. A return to health, a chance to make amends, a possibility of turning things around. I want this book to get that message across. Addiction is a disease, and it is an illness of the mind, body and spirit. When it is active, it is vile and hugely destructive. In recovery, the possibilities of life present themselves once again. Truth and beauty have a chance to shine.

Resources

1 *Alcoholics Anonymous (third edition)* - AA World Service Inc.

2 *Addiction as a Disease*, David R Hughes 1997 www.medicalonline.com/addict.htm

3 Internet Article, American Society of Addiction Medicine
   Definition of Addiction - Public Policy Statement 2010

4 *Pleasures Unwoven*, Kevin McCauley, 2009

5 *The House I Live in*, Eugene Jarecki, 2012

6 *I'll Quit Tomorrow* and *Intervention*, Vernon E Johnson

7 *Intervention and Families*, Bill Stevens bill@redchair.co.uk

8 www.tdpf.org.uk

9 *Chasing The Scream*, Johann Hari

10 *One Breath at a Time*, Kevin Griffin

11 *Addictive Thinking*, Abraham J Twerski MD

12 Contact me at sarina.wheatman2@gmail.com